fishin' LINES

This book is dedicated to those determined fishermen who go out and fish for the sport of it — and also to those who occasionally catch something.

Especially for:

Illustrations by Peter T. Secker

Behold the fisherman: he riseth up in the morning and disturbeth all; mighty are his preparations; he goeth forth full of hope— and when his day is spent, he returneth, smelling of strong drink; and the truth is not in him.

Fish: an animal
that goes on
vacation about the
same time
fishermen do.

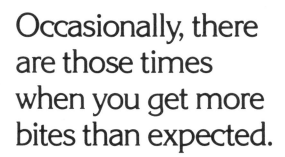

Occasionally, there
are those times
when you get more
bites than expected.

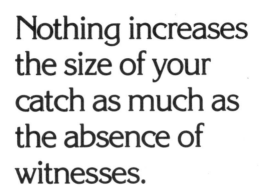

Nothing increases
the size of your
catch as much as
the absence of
witnesses.

To be a success at
fishing you should
get there yesterday,
when the fish were
biting.

Don't you wish you had three hands?

9

The three B's of fishing:

- **Boat**
- **Bait**
- **Beer**

10

Fishing, with me,
has always been an
excuse to drink in
the daytime.

—Jimmy Cannon

How far a fisherman
stretches the truth
depends on the
length of his arms.

Many a problem
will solve itself if
we forget it and
go fishing.

14

George Washington
was not a fisherman
—he never told a lie!

"I lost my rod."

Criterion by which lost fish are described:

A. Flash of scales. . ."Monster"

B. Light nibble. . . ."Lunker"

C. Tug on line. . . . ."Whopper"

D. Broken line. . . . ."World record"

Hot spot: where a particular species of fish was last week.

Fishing fanatic: an individual whose concentration is not swayed by surrounding distractions.

Fisherman: a sportsman who first lies in wait for a fish, and then lies in weight after catching it.

Most fishermen find
it impossible to keep
both hands in their
pockets while
describing the fish
that got away.

Fishing: a sport played with a long pole that has a worm at one end and a fool at the other.

How come the fish
never brags about
the size of the man
he got away from?

Fishing Rules of Thumb:

A. Never have a witness to the lunker that got away.

B. Never go the day after your neighbor "slayed 'em."

C. Never fish with a minister.

Henry tries the more direct approach!

Work: a dangerous disorder affecting high public functionaries who want to go fishing.

—Ambrose Bierce

Nothing grows
faster than a fish
from the time he
bites until the time
he gets away.

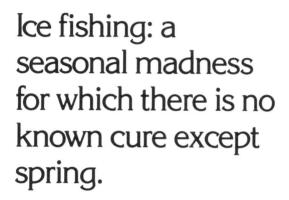

Ice fishing: a
seasonal madness
for which there is no
known cure except
spring.

Men have three secret wishes—to outsmart racehorses, women and fish.

34

Nothing makes a
fish bigger than
almost being
caught.

Then there are those
times when you can
swear you've got a
fish, but all you've
caught is weeds.

Fishing is like
romance—the next
best thing to
experiencing it
is talking about it.

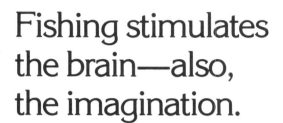

Fishing stimulates
the brain—also,
the imagination.

39

Fishing is a sport that makes men and truth strangers.

Fishing is the art
of doing almost
nothing.

Shirley Duffnagle's
fear about going to
the bathroom over
the side of the boat
comes true.

Fishing is a laborious way of taking it easy.

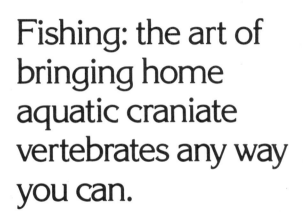

Fishing: the art of
bringing home
aquatic craniate
vertebrates any way
you can.

45

Fishing fanatic: one who refuses to don the proper attire on those rare days when he makes it to the office.

License: a permit issued that allows fishermen to drink beer and swear in a specific area.

It's always good
fishing just before
you get there.

Another day,
another shutout.

It's the innovative
fisherman who will
use his beer bottle
for a bobber.

The typical
fisherman is long on
optimism and short
on memory.

53

Never, never tackle more than you can handle!

55

I fish just
for the halibut.

THE TEN
COMMANDMENTS
OF FISHING

COMMANDMENT

Thou shalt not covet thy neighbor's fish.

COMMANDMENT

Thou shalt only use regulation approved fishing equipment.

COMMANDMENT

T hou shalt not use faulty rulers when measuring keepers.

Thou shalt not use too limber a rod when casting.

Thou shalt not sit on one's lure!

Thou shalt only fish in open water.

When frustrated, thou shalt not pop a wheelie in the boat.

VIII
COMMANDMENT

Thou shalt only fish for creatures without arms and legs.

COMMANDMENT

IX

Thou shalt not troll at excessive speeds.

Thou shalt not inflate the truth.

Other Golf Gifts Products:

- *The Complete Golfer's Handbook*
- *100 Sure Ways to Sharpen Your Game*
- *Golf Quotes*
- *The Ladies Tee*
- *Games Golfers Play*
- Scoring Log
- *Golf Tips*
- Golf Diary
- Links to the Past
- Ball Marker Collector
- Tee-Cup
- Pocket Pointers®
- *Birdies in the Oven*

- *Aces in the Kitchen*
- Behold the Golfer
- Party-Pak
- Golf Napkins
- Collectible Prints
- Brass Golf Plaques
- Golf Notes
- Towel Caddie
- T-Marks
- "In the Rough" Greeting Cards
- Holiday Cards
- *The Trouble with Tennis*
- *Fishing Lines*

GOLF GIFTS INC.
880 Oak Creek Drive • Lombard, IL 60148
1-800-552-4430 • (708) 953-9087

ISBN: 0-931089-96-4   Printed in Hong Kong